Romance at Camelot

by
Mervyn Whittaker

Cornelsen

Romance at Camelot

im Auftrag des Verlages erarbeitet von
Mervyn Whittaker

in Zusammenarbeit mit der Verlagsredaktion
Susanne Self

Titelbild und Illustration
Robert Broomfield, Tunbridge Wells

Technische Umsetzung
Knut Waisznor

Cornelsen online http://www.cornelsen.de

1. Auflage Druck 10 9 8 7 Jahr 06 05 04 03

Alle Drucke dieser Auflage sind inhaltlich unverändert und können im Unterricht nebeneinander verwendet werden.

Druck: Saladruck, Berlin

ISBN 3-464-05327-X

Bestellnummer 53270

Gedruckt auf säurefreiem Papier, umweltschonend hergestellt aus chlorfrei gebleichten Faserstoffen.

Contents

I
The Round Table

King Arthur stood at the top of his great Castle of Camelot. He was looking out of the window over his Kingdom of Logres and remembering. He had not had an easy time when he had become king. Britain was not a peaceful place then, because the Saxons were always fighting against Arthur's people. And that was not all: the British lords and princes were fighting each other, too.

So one day, Merlin, the wise old magician, told the people of Britain, "This must stop. Arthur is your king. Remember, he was the only man who was able to pull the sword out of the stone in London." And the people remembered this test and said, "Yes, you're right, he must be our king." But still Arthur had to prove that he was a champion knight. He showed that in the many battles against the Saxons and against the British knights which he won and in the many good deeds that he did. And always his friend Merlin and the magic sword Excalibur helped him.

And now Arthur went to his friend, for he had decided something. "Merlin," he said, "the time has come and I must have a wife. And I know who she will be, too: I want Guinevere, I have seen her and she is the most beautiful woman in the world." But Merlin could see into the future, and he told the young king: "That means trouble, I'm afraid. You will not be the only man who loves her; the best knight at your court will love her too, and war will follow."

But the king thought only of Guinevere, and when Merlin told her father, of course he was very glad for his daughter. So Arthur invited all the best knights and lords of the kingdom to the wedding at Camelot.

When they were preparing for the wedding, Arthur thought of a problem: "All my guests are very proud knights and great lords," he said to Merlin. "And only some of them can sit at the

top of the table, but the others will be angry, won't they?" Merlin listened and smiled and only said, "Leave that to me." So there was a great wedding with guests from all over the Kingdom of Logres, the best knights and their ladies. And when they all returned from church to the feasting hall, they saw the biggest round table they had ever seen with 150 chairs around it. So nobody was at the top of the table and each knight was the same in honour.

"Please sit down," said King Arthur, and his friend Merlin began to speak to the great guests. "This," he said, "is the first day of the Round Table. Even a thousand years from now, people will speak of us all here together in Camelot. For it is only the best knights who can sit down at this table, and they may only take a chair if their name is written in golden letters on its back." And all the knights looked behind them and saw that this was true, their names were there in golden letters. Merlin went on. "In future, you will meet around this table every year, and news of the Round Table will reach everybody in Britain. But you won't just sit here. For every true knight loves adventures, and no feast at the Round Table will begin without an exciting adventure."

He had not finished speaking when the first adventure started. Suddenly, the door opened and different animals ran around the hall. Then a lady came in and cried for help. Finally, a strange knight rode in, lifted the lady up and went off quickly on his horse. Three of the best knights – Sir Gawain, Sir Tor and King Pellinore – followed them. When they returned to the feast, they told everybody of their many and dangerous adventures and the other knights of the Round Table admired them for the good deeds they had done.

"And so it will always be," said Merlin, "you need never wait long for adventure when you sit down in the hall. And remember – as Knights of the Round Table, you must do your best in everything. You must never hurt anybody except in a

fair battle; you must always be true; if you see someone who needs your help, you must help him all you can; and to ladies especially you must be polite and good."

These were the last words that Merlin spoke at Camelot. When the old magician had to say goodbye, King Arthur was the saddest man of all. "You can't leave me here alone!" he said. But Arthur was a man now, and could well be king alone.

So why did Merlin have to go? Well, the reason was a lady from the magic Land of the Lake. Her name was Lady Nimue, and she could do the strongest magic. Her magic was even stronger than Merlin's, and the old man had to follow her. She took him into the hills of Wales, and there, somewhere, she led him down some stairs that went into the ground. Then she made the old magician sleep.

And many people say he is still sleeping there today, somewhere in the hills of Wales. But they say, too, that he might return one day to help people again with his magic.

II
Sir Gawain and the Green Knight

The news of the Round Table brought many knights to Camelot who wanted to test King Arthur and his guests to see if it was true that the Knights of the Round Table loved adventures and were not afraid of danger when people needed their help. So one day, when everybody was just sitting down to feast in the hall, the door suddenly flew open and a very tall man on a great horse rode in. Nobody in the hall knew him. He looked very strong, but strangest of all was that he and his horse were both green from head to foot; the knight's clothes were green, his hair was green, his face was green; and his horse was as green as he was.

The Knights of the Round Table were so surprised that they only looked and listened when the Green Knight started to talk in a loud, strict voice. "So you are the Knights of the Round Table, are you? People say you are the best in the world. I'm going to test your courage, and see if you will agree to a dangerous adventure. Look, here is my axe" – and he showed everybody a great green and golden axe. "I will fight with this axe against any man in this hall. I will stand first, and your knight may hit me with the axe as hard as he likes. But – listen carefully – when one year has gone by, that knight must come to meet me and then I will be allowed to hit first."

Now it became very quiet in the great hall. The Green Knight looked round him. He was just beginning to laugh at King Arthur's men when somebody said, "I will do it!" It was Sir Gawain, one of the first and best knights at the Round Table. King Arthur was his uncle, and he was very worried about the danger. But Sir Gawain stood up and said, "Come, sir, give me your axe!"

When Sir Gawain had taken it, the Green Knight got off his horse and prepared himself. He brushed his long green hair from his neck and then did not move while he waited. Gawain

was a strong man, and he wanted to win this dangerous fight at once. So he lifted the axe, swung back and hit the strange knight as hard as he could on the neck. The axe cut the green head clean off and it rolled across the hall.
But the Green Knight only stood up, went after his head and took it under his arm. "Well done, good knight," the head said. "But remember, in one year from today it is my turn. I am the Knight of the Green Chapel and you will find me in the Forest of Wirral in Wales. Meet me there." And he was gone.

King Arthur was white. "This is terrible, Gawain – you must not go!" But Sir Gawain only answered, "I will go, for I must show the world that I am a true knight."
And one year later, with a heavy heart, he went looking for the Green Knight in the Forest of Wirral.
He rode through the forest all day and all night, and when it was evening again he saw a castle and asked if he could sleep there. The lord of the castle was a tall and friendly man. "You must be my guest of honour!" he said. After dinner he asked,

"Where are you going?" "To the Green Chapel," said Gawain, "and I must be there in three days." – "Well, you can stay in my castle for those three days," said the lord, "for the chapel is very near here."

They drank together and when it was late, the lord laughed a lot and said, "Listen, I'm going hunting tomorrow. But you can stay in bed and sleep long. And, just for fun, let's make a promise: I'll give you whatever I get while I'm hunting, and you give me whatever you get here." And both of them laughed more and promised each other these presents.

When Sir Gawain opened his eyes next morning, the lady of the castle came quietly into his bedroom and sat down on his bed. "Good morning, Sir Knight of the Round Table," she said to him, and he thought to himself, "What a beautiful woman she is!" But he only said, "Good morning to you." She talked of this and that, and Gawain remembered Merlin's last words

and tried to be very polite to her. But soon she started to speak words of love. So the knight said, "My lady, you are the wife of the lord of the castle, and I am his guest. You may not speak like that." But the lady only laughed and said, "Ah, you could ask for one little kiss from me!" Gawain thought this was all right and he took her kiss.

In the evening, the lord returned and brought Gawain all the animals he had hunted. "And what did you win today?" laughed the lord. "One kiss," said Gawain. "Oh, who from?" – "No, I needn't tell you that! That wasn't our promise!" and both men spent the evening together and feasted.

The same thing happened the next day. Gawain opened his eyes and saw the lady, even more beautiful than the first day – and when the evening came, he gave the lord of the castle two kisses, and got presents from the hunt and they laughed and feasted together the whole evening.

The third morning, the sun was shining into his bedroom and the lovely lady of the castle spoke so sweetly to Sir Gawain that he nearly forgot to be a true knight. So she could give him three kisses this time, but still she said, "Gawain, are you really one of the best men at Arthur's court? It can't be so, for you would love me then!" Now she looked him in the eyes. "Gawain, please do this for me; take this green lace as a present from me, and wear it, so that you will always think of me." At first, he did not want to, but she said, "You can't say no, please wear it. But you won't tell my husband about it, will you?" And Gawain didn't. That evening, he gave the lord of the castle the three kisses, but he hid the green lace.

In the morning, the two friends said goodbye, for it was the day when Gawain had to meet the Green Knight. He had not gone far when he arrived at the Green Chapel, and there was the sound of somebody who was making an axe ready for battle. "Here I am, Sir Gawain of the Round Table," called the knight. Then he saw the terrible man again he had seen one year ago – the same green face and green hair.

"All right, Gawain, it's my turn today and my axe is ready. Leave your horse at that tree, stand here on the ground and don't move." – "Of course I won't move," said Gawain. "Who do you think I am?" And the tall strong knight lifted the axe and swung very near to Gawain's head – but he did not hit him. "Now I will do better," said the Green Knight and swung the axe again. Gawain did not move, but the axe did not touch him either. "But now I will cut off your head," spoke the green man. This time, he really cut Gawain's neck and blood came out. But it only hurt a little and he was not badly injured.
The Green Knight put down the axe and suddenly started to speak in a friendly way. "Sir Gawain, you have done well, and that is the reason why I decided not to cut off your head. You are a true knight and you kept your promises in the castle. You gave me all the kisses you got from my wife on the first, the second and the third day." – "So you are ..." began Gawain, "... but listen, sir, I am not really a good knight, for I didn't keep my promise on the last day. I must show you this green lace which I hid and ..." – "I know, Gawain, my wife told me everything. I knew that you had hidden the green lace from me and I made you pay for it with your blood. Keep the green lace to remember your adventure." – "But, my lord of the castle, how can you change like this?" asked Sir Gawain. "I must tell you that I got this magic from Lady Nimue, the Lady of the Lake. She sent me to test the Knights of the Round Table."
And once again he laughed loudly and said goodbye, while Gawain went home to King Arthur to tell his story.

III

Lancelot becomes a knight

Some of the chairs of the Round Table were still empty, and others became empty when their owners fell in battle. But there were always enough proud young men who wanted to become one of Arthur's knights. Of these, Lancelot of the Lake was the best.

He was called "of the Lake" because, as a child, he had lived in the magic Land of the Lake. Nimue, the Lady of the Lake, had looked after him. Now that Lancelot was a man, she took him to Camelot to King Arthur's great hall. "I bring you a new knight, Arthur. Before Merlin went under the ground, he told me I must lead Lancelot to you. Look – already his name is appearing in golden letters on that chair!"

The guests at the table were surprised and excited to see the new name and even more to see the young man, who was wonderful to look at. Queen Guinevere especially lost all the colour from her face as she watched the beautiful young man take his chair. When Lancelot saw Queen Guinevere he thought that she was the most wonderful woman in the world. At that moment they both knew that they loved each other. King Arthur gave Lancelot a warm welcome and, without any more questions, made him a Knight of the Round Table.

Now, this annoyed some of the older knights. "Who does he think he is?" Sir Kay angrily asked his neighbour. "He has fought no battles and has had no adventures, he is no more than a boy, and already a knight! It's not right!" (In fact, Sir Kay himself was not exactly the best of the knights and he was jealous of Lancelot.) Sir Lancelot heard the trouble among the knights, and he knew he was as good as any of them; he only had to show it. "I will leave King Arthur's court," he thought to himself, "and I will find adventures which will prove my courage to the world. ... And perhaps they will help me forget Queen Guinevere."

The next year, all the adventures were his. But it would take too long to tell them all: How he healed an injured knight when he touched him with his hand; how he fought the wicked knight Sir Turquyn and so saved his brother Sir Hector from prison; or how four beautiful queens tried to win his love. The year was nearly over when Lancelot decided to return to Camelot for the feast.

On his way, he met a lady who was standing under a great tree and crying. "Oh, dear Lancelot," she cried, "you are the best knight in the land. Look up there, my husband's hawk is caught at the top of the tree. If I come home without it, he will do something terrible to me. You must help me!" Lancelot did not think twice but took off his armour and climbed the tree.

Half way up, he suddenly heard a man on the ground who was laughing loudly at him. "Ha, ha, ha, Sir Lancelot," laughed the false knight, "now I've got you without your armour and without your sword. This will be the end of you!" – "Sir Knight!" said Lancelot. "You know that isn't a fair battle. Let me go." But the knight only waited for him, with his sword ready in his hand.

Then Sir Lancelot suddenly thought of something. He broke a large piece of dead wood from the tree and jumped to the ground. "Now you can fight with me," he said. The false knight ran at Lancelot and tried to hit his unprotected body with his sword. But Lancelot was too quick for him. He threw his heavy piece of wood so hard against the knight's head that even his armour was no help to him. For a moment, the knight let his sword fall. Lancelot quickly took it, and before the knight could remember where he was and throw his spear at him, Lancelot cut off his head.

"My husband – he's dead! You wicked, wicked knight, Lancelot!" cried the lady. "It was him or me," said Sir Lancelot. "You both wanted me dead, didn't you?" and he rode away.

That night, Lancelot was just going to bed in a castle near Camelot when he heard loud shouts. He looked out of the window and saw Sir Kay on one side of a field and three knights on the other. "Oh no!" thought Lancelot. "He's in bad trouble!" And he quickly put his armour on again and rode to the field of battle. "Turn round!" he called, and at once the three knights lifted their swords against him, and the battle started. But in the end, only Lancelot was still on his horse, while the three knights were glad they still had their lives. Lancelot looked at the frightened Sir Kay, smiled and said, "Listen, you three knights: Go to Camelot Castle and give yourselves up to King Arthur, and tell him this: 'Sir Kay sent us'." The knights did not want to do so, for Kay was no fighter, but they remembered Lancelot's strict words and went.
Sir Kay thanked Sir Lancelot and both spent the night in the castle. In the morning, Lancelot saw that the other knight was still sleeping, and he had an idea. "What a good joke it would

be to wear Sir Kay's armour and to ride into Camelot as Sir Kay. Then nobody will recognize me or him. Let's see what will happen!"

He rode away, and Sir Kay of course had to put on Lancelot's armour. Kay did not mind; in fact he really enjoyed riding into Camelot like that. No other knight stopped him or annoyed him. It was the first time that he arrived home without any trouble.

But Lancelot had his fun, too. Lots of knights shouted, "Look, here comes proud Sir Kay! Let's see if he is as good as he always says he is!" And they rode against the knight, ready for a nice, easy fight. They were very surprised when he knocked them off their horses, and they lay on the ground, their legs in the air, and asked themselves what had happened.

Next day, the Knights of the Round Table came together again, and Sir Kay told the story of how he had ridden home in peace while Lancelot had played a joke on so many knights who came to fight with him. Then everybody laughed, King Arthur most of all. Sir Hector told how Lancelot had rescued him and some other Knights of the Round Table from prison. And still there was more talk of this young knight's dangerous and successful adventures.

This time, Sir Lancelot had the greatest name of all the knights, and nobody talked any more about a boy who had become a knight for nothing.

IV
Morgan le Fay and Lady Ragnell

When King Arthur had brought peace to the Kingdom of Logres, he still had no peace for himself. He knew that trouble was waiting for him wherever he went, and his life was not safe. His half-sister, Morgan le Fay, was the reason for this trouble. She hated Arthur and she had made a promise that she would kill him one day. Worse than that, Morgan had learnt very strong magic, which gave her great power over people and things. So she was very dangerous, as this story will show.

One day, King Arthur was in battle with a knight called Gromer Somer Joure, when suddenly he could fight no longer. A magic power had stopped his hand. The knight lifted his sword to kill him. "This is the devil's work!" cried Arthur. "I can't move!" – "Not the devil's work," laughed Gromer Somer Joure, "only your sister's, Morgan le Fay's. But, poor King, I won't kill you now, I'll give you a second chance. Listen: I'll ask you a difficult riddle and you may have one year to find the answer. After that year, you must promise to come back here." King Arthur promised and the knight told him the riddle: "What is it that women want more than anything else in the world? You go and find the answer to that!"

For the next twelve months, the king rode across the land and tried to find the answer. He knew that without it, he would soon be dead. He asked many people and heard many answers, but he was not sure if he had found the right answer. The day before his meeting with Gromer Somer Joure, he was riding through the forest when suddenly a person stood in his way. There was a scream, "Stop, King Arthur!"

Arthur and his knights stopped and looked at the person. And their eyes grew wide. It was a lady, but the ugliest lady they had ever seen. She was very fat, had a face like a fish and hair like grass; when she spoke, it was like a dog with a cold. Even the horses walked backwards when they saw her.

"Stop and listen, King. My name is Lady Ragnell and I can help you. I know the answer that can save your life. The answer to Sir Gromer's riddle." King Arthur suddenly became excited. "Quickly, woman, what is it?" – "Not so fast, sir. I'll tell you the answer when you have promised me something." – "All right, what?" asked Arthur. "I want one of your knights to be my husband," said the ugly lady in her strange voice. All the knights went back even further when they heard this. "But I can't ...," began King Arthur.

Now Sir Gawain, the best of the knights, felt a little sorry for his king, who would die without the answer, and perhaps he felt sorry for Lady Ragnell, too. "I will be her husband!" he said. "No, you mustn't, that is too hard for you!" cried Arthur. But Sir Gawain only said, "Speak no more. I'm serious." And so King Arthur finally agreed to the promise and the lady whispered the answer to the riddle in his ear. "It's not difficult if you think about it," she added with a little laugh.

The king returned to Gromer Somer Joure. "Well, I'm listening," said the knight when they met in the darkest part of the forest. "This is the answer," spoke Arthur. "What women want more than anything else in the world is to have their own way." – "You have found the right answer," said the knight. "I will not hurt you. Believe me, I am a true knight who keeps his word. I do not hate you – only Morgan's magic made me fight you." Arthur rode home, a free man.

But for Sir Gawain, the problems were just beginning. When they rode into Camelot, King Arthur, Sir Gawain and Lady Ragnell, all the people along the way were happy to see their king again and shouted and laughed. But when they saw the woman at Gawain's side, they were suddenly quiet and had to look away. Gawain, too, was sad when he thought about the future with his wife.

But he had given his word as a knight and so he married her the same day. Nobody enjoyed the wedding or the feast in the great hall of Camelot. All the knights and ladies liked Sir

Gawain and they whispered to each other, "How terrible for the poor young man! How terrible she looks when she is eating and drinking at table! And poor Gawain must listen to her when she speaks in that strange, loud voice, too!"

Slowly Sir Gawain followed Lady Ragnell to bed that night. "And now," she shouted, "you must kiss me! You are my husband and I'm your wife, you know!" The knight wanted to turn away and forget her, but he remembered his promise. And again, he felt a little sorry for her, because he sometimes saw in her eyes that she looked – frightened.

He came nearer and nearer to her face and finally kissed her. At once he let her go and went to the window and put his hands over his face and cried.

But what was this? Behind him he heard a sweet, quiet voice which said, "Gawain. My dear Lord Gawain!" He turned round and saw the loveliest girl that he had ever seen. She watched him with her face full of love. "But ... but, who are you? And where is my wife Ragnell?" he asked. "I am Lady Ragnell, and

your wife, if you want to have me." Gawain did not know if he was more surprised or more happy at how she had changed. "You see," she went on, "the wicked Queen Morgan le Fay used magic on me and my brother Gromer Somer Joure. And she changed me into that ugly woman. Because you felt sorry for me and made me your wife, Gawain, that magic is broken." Gawain could say nothing.

"But there is still a problem. You see, I may only be in my true form for twelve hours every day, and then I must become ugly again for twelve hours. So what shall I do? You must say which you want. If I am ugly by day, all the knights and ladies here in Camelot will talk and whisper about you with me at your side. But if I change into my terrible form in the evening, just think: When you are alone with me after a long day has gone by, you must listen to my awful voice and I will give you no peace. So choose carefully."

"No," said Gawain after a moment. "You must decide. It is more terrible for you. Just imagine – how sad you will be when I am near you at night and I cannot touch you or kiss you. Or during the day, when nobody will talk to you, and the children at Camelot will run after you and laugh. Oh, my dear lady, you must choose."

Lady Ragnell threw her arms round Sir Gawain's neck and kissed him. A minute later, she was dancing happily around her new husband. "Now the magic is finished for ever. As you see me now, so I will be your wife both day and night for many happy years. You have given me what every woman wants – her own way! You broke the magic with your answer."

Next day, there was a real feast at Camelot Castle. The hall was full of music and food, drink and noise, as everybody celebrated the happiest husband and wife at the Round Table – and their victory over Queen Morgan le Fay.

V
Perceval becomes a knight

Perceval never knew his father. His mother took him into the forest when he was a baby and hid with him there. Perceval's mother never talked to her son about his father, a great knight who had died in battle. She wanted to keep Perceval away from the world of knights and kings and so she only taught him about the King of Heaven. For fifteen years, Perceval saw no other person and learnt nothing of the world outside the forest. But he grew and became a tall and strong man who could run fast and hunt for his mother and himself.

So it happened that he was hunting in the forest one day when he met five knights in shining armour who were riding there. His eyes nearly fell out of his head. "Hello, young man," laughed their leader, Sir Lancelot. "Have you never seen a

knight before?" Perceval thought that the knights in their bright armour were the most wonderful thing he had ever seen. "Are you from the Kingdom of Heaven?" he asked, for his mother had told him what a wonderful place the Kingdom of Heaven was. "Well, yes, we are for the King of Heaven, too," said Lancelot. "But our king is Arthur – he made us knights. And," he went on with a little joke, "if you come to Camelot, perhaps he will make you one, too!" And they laughed as they continued their journey.

But Perceval, when he returned to his mother, could speak only of one thing – of knights and Camelot. His mother cried because she knew she must lose him now, and she said her words of goodbye to him: "Go on your way now, for you are ready for the world. Many things you still must learn, but the King of Heaven will always be with you, and deep inside of you you will always know what is right and what is wrong."

Perceval had not gone far when he came to a field with a beautiful red and golden tent in the middle. He was curious to see more, for there was nobody near it. He thought it was a church for he had never seen one before. So he put his head in and looked around. Now he was looking at something else he had never seen before; a beautiful girl was sleeping quietly there. She was so lovely that he went nearer.

He felt she was so wonderful, he must have something that would make him think of her always, so he took her ring from her finger and put his own ring on hers. Then he quickly kissed her before he walked out of the tent and on to Camelot.

King Arthur and his knights were just sitting down to their feast at the Round Table when Perceval arrived and stood quietly in a corner of the hall to watch. At the same moment, a loud voice shouted from outside, "Let me come in! I'm the Red Knight!" The knights were very annoyed because they wanted to start to drink to each other. "That's all you can do – eat and drink!" cried the Red Knight, inside the hall now. "Well, I want some too!" With that, he took a heavy golden cup from the table and drank it empty. "I have taken your cup," he said to King Arthur, "and soon I will take your land, too." Then he turned round, the cup still in his hand, and rode away.

"Well, I never ...!" began the king, very angrily. "Who will bring me back my cup and teach this man a lesson?" Every knight wanted this adventure for himself. But Arthur said, "No, a knight is too good for this silly man. Listen: if there is a young man in this hall who wants to become a knight, let him follow that man. And if he comes back in the Red Knight's armour, I will make him a knight."

At once Perceval asked for a horse and followed the enemy, while Sir Kay watched him and said, "You've got no chance, boy. With no armour and only that spear made of wood in your hand, the Red Knight will make cat's meat out of you!"

Perceval rode quickly and soon saw the Red Knight, who was going up a hill not far away. "Turn round, knight, and meet your death!" called the boy. Now the Red Knight got ready, held his great spear in his hand and rode down the hill at Perceval. The boy waited while the man got faster and faster, nearer and nearer. Then, at the last moment, he quickly jumped to one side. The knight could not stop so fast, of course, so he went on down the hill at top speed. Now he was angry. "I'll get you this time! You'll be dead in a minute, boy!" he shouted and shook his spear. He hit his horse to make it run faster. Perceval was ready for him. He waited until the knight had come next to him, pushed his great spear away and threw his own spear at the knight. The throw was so clever and so powerful that it went through a hole in the Red Knight's armour and into his neck. He fell off the horse and lay there, dead.

Now Perceval started his next job; he had to take the Red Knight's armour off. The problem was, Perceval had no idea how to put armour on or how to take it off. He turned it round this way and that to see where it opened. But it was no use. He could not get the armour off. Just at that moment an old man came along the way and asked what he was doing. "I want to get this man out of his armour and wear it myself because I want to become a knight." – "Oh, dear," said the nice old man, whose name was Gonemans. "Let me show you," and he helped the boy. After that day, Perceval stayed with Gonemans for six months. The old man taught him all the things he had to know as a knight: how to wear his armour and sit on a horse, how to be polite to ladies and to keep his honour in all his deeds. Together they practised how to fight. Then Perceval again got on his horse, this time in his bright armour, and rode away to return to King Arthur and become a knight.

But the strangest of adventures happened to him in a castle on the way back to Camelot. He really only went in to spend the night there, but before he came out again the next morning, he had seen three wonderful sights which he would never forget. The first thing he saw was a game of chess that was standing on a table. He was curious and so he played and moved the white pieces. But the strange thing was, the black pieces moved on their own, by magic. Perceval played many games against the magic hand, but he lost them all. He was so angry that he wanted to break the chess game up, but a voice said, "Stop, Perceval; don't do that!" He turned round and saw the girl from the tent whom he had kissed. She was looking even more beautiful than he remembered her. Before, he had not known what he had felt; now, he knew that he loved her. She told him that her name was Blanchefleur, "White Flower". "I'm still wearing your ring, Perceval," she said and showed her hand. Perceval was happy and showed her his hand, too.

The third thing Perceval saw in this strange castle was perhaps the most wonderful of all: With Blanchefleur at his side, he had a vision of the Holy Grail, which came to him in the brightest light a person had ever seen. This wonderful Grail was a vision of the cup which Jesus had used on the night before he died. Blanchefleur told him that only the truest knights could ever drink out of it. Perceval wanted to take the cup, but before he

could touch it, it was gone. When he turned round, Blanchefleur was gone, too.

Still full of his wonderful adventures, he returned to Camelot and told about all he had done and seen. There was no question: Perceval deserved to become a knight, and King Arthur showed him his place at the Round Table. In fact, the golden letters of his name had already been on his chair for nearly a year.

But Perceval could not forget Blanchefleur and his vision of the Holy Grail. He did not stay at Camelot long, but went back out into the world and tried to find them.

VI
Lancelot and Guinevere

Many years later, King Arthur and Queen Guinevere still held their feasts at the Round Table, but the hall was getting emptier. The battles and adventures had killed many knights, and there were not so many new knights to fill their places. Some years before, several of King Arthur's knights had ridden away to find the Holy Grail, but only Sir Perceval, Sir Bors and Sir Galahad had seen it, the best of the knights. Sir Galahad, the son of Lancelot, was the truest of them all, and he not only looked on the Grail, but was even allowed to drink out of it.

Sir Lancelot himself had tried hard to find the Grail, but he never did. Deep inside him, he knew the reason: He still loved Guinevere as he had loved her the first day he saw her, and she loved him. But Guinevere was his queen and the wife of his lord, and Lancelot knew that this love was wrong.

So he tried to stay away from her and to go out on adventures to forget her. "Lancelot," she said to him one day, "I see you are always riding away to help ladies and girls who are in danger. And you don't come near me any more. Have you found a woman you love more than me, perhaps?" – "I never have and never will," spoke the knight. "Those are not true words, Lancelot. You are tired of me and have found somebody else. Go away and never come near me again!"

But both were crying when they left each other.

A week later, Queen Guinevere called the girls at Camelot together to celebrate May Day, like they did every year. It was wonderful to see the group of young ladies, who were wearing only white and had put the first flowers of spring in their hair, as they laughed and had fun while they followed their queen into the fresh, green forest. Deep in the forest, they enjoyed their dances in the grass between the trees and spent the night in a large and beautiful blue and white tent.

They did not know it, but they were not alone. A false knight called Sir Melliagraunce was watching from behind a tree. For a long time, he had loved Queen Guinevere, and now he saw his chance to take her and lead her to his castle. Although she cried for help, the bad knight with his many men were too strong for her and they carried her off with her girls. Only one was able to escape. She ran back to Camelot to tell Arthur.

The first person she met there was Sir Lancelot. He had not been able to stay away from the court of his queen any longer and had returned. As soon as he heard the news, he jumped on his horse. “If I don't come back,” he called to King Arthur, “you will know that Melliagraunce has killed me.” Arthur only shook his head sadly and said he was very disappointed at Sir Melliagraunce, who was a Knight of the Round Table.

“Come out and fight!” shouted Lancelot when he got to the castle where the knight was keeping Guinevere, for he was ready to cut Melliagraunce in pieces. But the queen was frightened for Lancelot: “Listen, good Lancelot; make peace with him now. As two Knights of the Round Table, you should wait and fight a fair battle before Arthur, your king.” Although Lancelot was very angry, both he and false Melliagraunce agreed to meet again a week later in Camelot.

After that, Melliagraunce seemed to be friendly to Lancelot and called him his guest, but it was only because he wanted to play a trick on him. He invited him into his castle, but then he threw him into prison.

On the day of the battle, all the knights and ladies, with King Arthur and Queen Guinevere in their middle, came out to watch the two knights. The field between Camelot and the river was full of people and lots of colours. “But where is Lancelot?” asked everybody. Sir Melliagraunce coughed, “Well, I suppose he must be too frightened to fight with me.” At that moment Lancelot, who had been able to break open a door and escape, rode into the field like a storm. “Let's see who is the chicken,” he said between his teeth. After that, Sir

Melliagraunce did not stay on his horse very long. In fact, he was lying flat on his back a minute later with Lancelot's foot on his neck.

The spectators celebrated the champion with loud shouts, but he only had ears for Guinevere, who whispered, "Meet me in the garden this afternoon."

It was the first warm day of the year and Queen Guinevere was waiting for him under an apple tree away from the sun when Sir Lancelot came into the garden. She looked at him with shining eyes. "Lancelot," she said, "after all these years you know and I know that Heaven made us for each other. I want you to come to my room tonight." Lancelot was unhappy; many things went through his head. "Must it be so?" he asked quietly. "You know it must," she said.

But three people, not just two, were in the garden that afternoon. The third was the terrible Sir Mordred, son of Morgan le Fay. He heard every word they said. "Ha, ha, now my chance has come," he laughed to himself and made his plans to

destroy the whole of Arthur's kingdom and to come to power himself. At once he collected some knights round him who were on his side. "Be ready tonight!" he told them.

They waited until Lancelot was in Guinevere's room and then stood in front of the door, fourteen men in armour with swords ready. "Come out, you false knight! We know you're in that bedroom with the queen. We're going to bring you before King Arthur!" Guinevere thought that their last moment had come, but Lancelot quickly held the door shut and said, "My Queen, have you got some armour for me? I have only my sword at my side." And to the knights he shouted, "Do you call this a fair fight, one man without armour against all of you?" But they did not listen.

Suddenly Lancelot had an idea. He put a thick piece of cloth round the arm without the sword and then quickly opened and shut the door so that only one of Mordred's men could come in. Then he hid behind the arm with the cloth and fought so cleverly with his sword that soon the man fell and moved no more. A moment later, Lancelot was wearing that knight's armour.

"Goodbye," Lancelot whispered to Guinevere, "and I promise, if you are in danger, I will be back!" With that, he threw the door open. He was fighting for his life as he cut his way through the thirteen knights, ran down to his horse and rode away into the night.

Mordred went straight to King Arthur and told him the story. "And your wife may not live," he said. "She has destroyed your honour and the honour of Camelot; and she is the reason for that poor knight's death." Sir Gawain and others tried to save her, for they knew that Arthur still loved her deeply. But in the end, the king said sadly, "There is no other way. The law says that a wife who has destroyed her husband's honour must be burnt to death."

Mordred was in a hurry to see her death, and not many days later he told some people to carry a lot of wood to the field where Melliagraunce and Lancelot had fought, and to tie the queen to a big piece of wood in the middle. The fire had already started to burn when suddenly a horse appeared out of nowhere, a sword knocked down several of King Arthur's men, a strong arm cut the queen free from the wood, and both the knight and the rescued queen escaped into the forest. Lancelot had kept his word.

But Lancelot and Guinevere could not enjoy their life together. In this second escape, Lancelot had killed more of the Knights of the Round Table, and he now had many enemies. Even Sir Gawain was against him now. Again and again Lancelot tried to make peace, for he felt sure King Arthur did not really want to fight him. He even gave Queen Guinevere back to her husband after he had promised to take her back in honour. But it was too late.

Sir Mordred's clever plans made each knight take sides against the others and hate them. Friends and even brothers died at each other's swords. Battles followed more battles. When Mordred himself was finally killed by Arthur in a last battle, the Kingdom of Logres was already in pieces.

And so the end of this story is a sad one. The Round Table in Camelot saw no more feasts, the golden names on the chairs were gone, and besides, there was nobody left to read them. King Arthur never returned to the castle which had once been the most famous in Europe, for he too was terribly injured in a battle after Morgan le Fay had destroyed the magic power of his sword Excalibur. As he was dying, Lady Nimue, so it is said, sent some women in a boat to take King Arthur to rest on an island in the magic Land of the Lake, the Island of Avalon.

Are they dead? Or just sleeping?

If you visit Britain one day, you may come to a place called Glastonbury, near the City of Wells in south-west England. There, you can see King Arthur's and Queen Guinevere's graves with your own eyes. In this village, the ruins of a great church stand today with grass all round them. And in the middle of the church's ruins, you will see a sign which says that the king and queen were buried here.

Some people say that is not true: It is Sir Lancelot and Queen Guinevere whose bones were laid in the ground here. For when King Arthur died, Guinevere turned away from this world and became a nun. Lancelot heard of that, saw that he could never win her, and became a monk. But they were not far away from each other, and when Guinevere finally died, Lancelot followed her just a few weeks later. The man and the woman who loved each other more than anybody else in the world finally came together when they were dead.

We just cannot know for sure what is true, for the stories of King Arthur and the Knights of the Round Table happened so many hundreds of years ago. So perhaps we should believe the story that tells us that King Arthur is not dead at all. He is only sleeping, like Merlin, and, like him, he is ready to come back and help Britain again when Britain needs him most.

Vocabulary

adj. = adjective, *n.* = noun, *sb.* = somebody, *sth.* = something

A (to) **admire** [əd'maɪə] bewundern
afraid: (to) **be afraid of** Angst haben vor
(to) **annoy sb.** jn. ärgern
among [ə'mʌŋ] (mitten) unter
any jede(r, s) (beliebige)
armour ['ɑːmə] Rüstung, Panzer
as soon as sobald
at first zuerst

B **backwards** ['bækwədz] rückwärts
besides [bɪ'saɪdz] außerdem
blood [blʌd] Blut
bone [bəʊn] Knochen
both day and night sowohl am Tag als auch in der Nacht
(to) **break up** abbrechen
buried: (to) **be buried** ['berɪd] begraben sein
burnt: (to) **be burnt** [bɜːnt] verbrannt werden

C (to) **carry sb. off** jn. entführen
(to) **celebrate** ['selɪbreɪt] feiern
champion (n.) ['tʃæmpjən] Sieger/in
champion (adj.) Meister-
(to) **change into** sich verwandeln in
chapel ['tʃæpl] Kapelle
chicken *auch:* Angsthase
cloth [klɒθ] Stoff
(to) **continue** [kən'tɪnjuː] fortsetzen

(to) **cough** [kɒf] husten
courage [ˈkʌrɪdʒ] Mut, Tapferkeit
(to) **cry for help** um Hilfe rufen
curious [ˈkjʊərɪəs] neugierig
(to) **cut sth. (off)** [kʌt], **cut** [kʌt], **cut** [kʌt] etwas (ab)schneiden
cut: he cut his way through er bahnte sich einen Weg durch

D **death** [deθ] Tod
deed [diːd] (Helden-)Tat
deep inside of you tief in dir
(to) **deserve** [dɪˈzɜːv] verdienen, verdient haben
devil [ˈdevl] Teufel
drink *auch:* Getränke
(to) **drink to each other** miteinander anstoßen

E **end: in the end** schließlich, am Ende
enemy [ˈenəmi] Feind/in
(to) **enjoy doing sth.** etwas (sehr) gerne tun
escape Flucht
Europe [ˈjʊərəp] Europa
excited [ɪkˈsaɪtɪd] aufgeregt, gespannt

F **false** [fɔːls] falsch, unaufrichtig
feast [fiːst] Festmahl, Festgelage
(to) **feast** ein Festmahl veranstalten, ein Festgelage halten
feasting hall Festsaal
fight Kampf
fighter [ˈfaɪtə] Kämpfer/in
(to) **finish doing sth.** aufhören, etwas zu tun

for denn
for ever für immer, ewig
for nothing umsonst
frightened erschreckt, erschrocken, verängstigt
frightened: (to) **be frightened for sb.** um jn. Angst haben
fun: (to) **have fun** Spaß haben, sich amüsieren

G **give up: give yourselves up to King Arthur** stellt euch (freiwillig) König Arthur
(to) **go out on adventures** Abenteuer suchen
golden [ˈgəʊldən] golden
gone verschwunden, weg(gegangen)
goodbye: words of goodbye Abschiedsworte
Grail → Holy Grail

H **half way up the tree** *hier:* als er halb oben auf dem Baum war
hawk [hɔːk] Habicht
(to) **heal** [hiːl] heilen
heart [hɑːt] Herz
heaven [ˈhevn] Himmel
hole [həʊl] Loch
Holy Grail [ˈhəʊlɪ ˈgreɪl] Gral *(Gefäß, aus dem Christus getrunken haben soll)*
honour [ˈɒnə] Ehre
hunt [hʌnt] Jagd
(to) **hunt** jagen

I **idea:** (to) **have no idea** keine Ahnung haben

J **jealous** ['dʒeləs] eifersüchtig, neidisch
joke → (to) **play a joke on sb.**
journey ['dʒɜːni] Reise

K (to) **keep** halten
Kingdom of Logres ['kɪŋdəm‿əv 'ləʊgrəs] Bezeichnung Englands zur Zeit König Arthurs
kiss Kuss
(to) **know** (sth.) **for sure** (etwas) sicher wissen, sicher sein

L **lace** [leis] Band
laugh Lachen
(to) **lead** [liːd], **led** [led], **led** [led] führen
leave that to me überlass das mir
led → (to) **lead**
left: (to) **be left** übrig sein
lesson: (to) **teach sb. a lesson** jm. eine Lektion erteilen
(to) **let** [let], **let** [let], **let** [let] lassen
Logres → **Kingdom of Logres**
(to) **look around** sich umsehen
love Liebe

M **magic** verzaubert, Zauber-
made of (wood) aus (Holz)
(to) **make sb. do sth.** jn. veranlassen/zwingen, etwas zu tun; jn. etwas tun lassen
(to) **make sb. sth.** jn. zu etwas machen
May Day ['meɪ deɪ] der erste Mai
(to) **mind** [maɪnd] etwas dagegen (einzuwenden) haben

monk [mʌŋk] Mönch
more than anybody else mehr als alle anderen
more than anything else mehr als alles andere

N **nobody talked any more about** niemand sprach mehr über
not ... any longer nicht länger
not ... any more nicht mehr
nun [nʌn] Nonne

O **on my/your own** allein, ohne Hilfe
once again noch einmal
one day eines Tages
out of nowhere aus dem Nichts
over: (to) **be over** vorüber sein

P **peaceful** friedlich
piece: in pieces zerfallen, kaputt
(to) **play a joke/trick on sb.** jm. einen Streich spielen
power Kraft, Macht
power: (to) **come to power** an die Macht gelangen
promise Versprechen
proud [praʊd] stolz
(to) **prove sth. to sb.** [pruːv] jm. etwas beweisen

Q **question: there was no question** es gab keinen Zweifel
question: without any more questions ohne weitere Fragen

R (to) **reach** [riːtʃ] erreichen
ready: (to) **get ready** sich fertig machen, sich bereitmachen
(to) **rest** [rest] (sich aus)ruhen
(to) **rescue** ['reskjuː] retten, befreien
riddle ['rɪdl] Rätsel
ring [rɪŋ] Ring
(to) **roll** [rəʊl] rollen
romance [rəʊ'mæns, 'rəʊmæns] (Liebes-)Abenteuer

S **said: it is said** man sagt
Saxon ['sæksn] (Angel-)Sachse/Sächsin
(to) **seem** [siːm] scheinen
serious: I'm serious ['sɪərɪəs] ich meine das im Ernst
shall: What shall I do? [ʃæl] Was soll ich tun?
shining ['ʃaɪnɪŋ] glänzend, leuchtend
sides: (to) **take sides against** Partei ergreifen gegen
(to) **smile** [smaɪl] lächeln
spear ['spɪə] Lanze, Speer
spectator [spek'teɪtə] Zuschauer/in
(to) **stay away from sb.** jn. meiden, jm. aus dem Wege gehen
straight direkt, unverzüglich
swing [swɪŋ], **swung** [swʌŋ], **swung** [swʌŋ] schwingen, (hin und her) schwenken
swung → (to) **swing**

T (to) **take off** *(Kleidung)* ausziehen
talk Gerede
(to) **test** auf die Probe stellen
(to) **thank** danken, sich bedanken (bei)
throw Wurf

tired: (to) **be tired of** überdrüssig sein
trick → (to) **play a trick on sb.**
true wahrhaftig, (ge)treu

U **unprotected** [ˌʌnprəʊˈtektɪd] ungeschützt
use: it was no use es hatte keinen Sinn

V **victory** [ˈvɪktəri] Sieg
vision [ˈvɪʒn] Vision, Phantasiebild
voice [vɔɪs] Stimme

W (to) **walk on to** weitergehen/weiterlaufen bis nach
(to) **watch sb. do(ing) sth.** beobachten, wie jd. etwas tut
way: her/their own way ihr eigener Wille
way: (to) **stand in sb.'s way** jm. im Wege stehen
wedding [ˈwedɪŋ] Hochzeit
whatever [wɒtˈevə] was (auch) immer
wherever [weərˈevə] wo(hin) (auch) immer
(to) **whisper** [ˈwɪspə] flüstern
whom [huːm] den, die, das; dem, der, dem *(Relativpronomen)*
wicked [ˈwɪkɪd] böse, bösartig, gemein
wide: their eyes grew wide [waɪd] sie rissen die Augen auf
wise [waɪz] weise
would [wʊd] würde

List of names

Arthur [ˈɑːθə]
Avalon [ˈævəlɒn]
Blanchefleur [ˈblɒːnʃˈflɜː]
Bors [bɔːs]
Camelot [ˈkæməlɒt]
Excalibur [ekˈskælɪbə]
Forest of Wirral [ˈfɒrɪst‿əv ˈwɪrəl]
Galahad [ˈgæləhæd]
Gawain [ˈgɑːweɪn]
Glastonbury [ˈglæstənbərɪ]
Gonemans [ˈgɒnɪməns]
Gromer Somer Joure [ˈgrʌmə sʌmə ˈdʒʊə]
Guinevere [ˈgwɪnɪvɪə]
Hector [ˈhektə]
Holy Grail [ˈhəʊlɪ ˈgreɪl]
Jesus [ˈdʒiːzəs]
Kay [keɪ]
Kingdom of Logres [ˈkɪŋdəm‿əv ˈləʊgrəs]
Lancelot [ˈlɑːnsəlɒt]
Melliagraunce [ˈmelɪəgrɔːns]
Merlin [ˈmɜːlɪn]
Mordred [ˈmɔːdrɪd]
Morgan le Fay [ˈmɔːgən lə ˈfeɪ]
Nimue [nɪˈmjuːɪ]
Pellinore [ˈpelɪnɔː]
Percevale [ˈpɜːsɪvəl]
Ragnell [ˈrægnəl]
Saxon [ˈsæksən]
Tor [tɔː]
Turquyn [ˈtɜːkwɪn]
Wales [weɪlz]
Wells [welz]